Speaking Kind Words

Speaking Kind Words

Improve your relationship with heartfelt words.

For the lover in all of us.

I am sure you have heard the old saying, "If you don't have anything nice to say, don't say anything at all." Well, what if you take that expression and put it to work improving your relationship? I am not saying that you can just speak nice words. Sometimes you need to be harsh even with your partner. However, you need to be compassionately harsh with him/her. It is important to understand the mental wellbeing of the person you are speaking to. Is she having trouble at work, is her health not the best it can be, or is he riding a high that you don't want to bring him down from? These are some of the questions you need to address before you let your partner know your feelings. Conversation is a wonderful thing and your conversation can be much better if your timing is right.

As you look through your day you can pick and choose times to say things to your partner. Far too often we all seem to have a habit of saying undesirable things right before we leave each other

– off to work, off to bed, off to the gym, off to the store. When we do this, maybe we are just trying to get that last word in. On the other hand, we tend to try to speak of positive or good things when we are going to be around each other for a while or when we want something from the other. This is because we want to bask in the glory of the kind words we speak.

The problem lies in that these events happen at totally random times. Due to this random timing there is no rhythm and we don't get a chance to expect kind words and praise from each other. The book you are holding in your hands is a wonderful tool to help change that. Following the guidelines within these pages you will find it easy to set up times and places where you can speak these kind heartwarming words. You will get to expect and enjoy the anticipation of the kind words that you know are coming.

This system is a tool to get you on the track of saying things that not only your partner will like to hear, but things that you would like to hear in return.   In the following pages there is a rotation of things to say to your partner to keep you from continually returning to the same old compliments. The reason for this is because if you continually speak of the same thing, those words lose their validity.   In those cases you are just going through the motions instead of truly speaking from your heart. There is a calendar in the back of this book that will lead you along the right path.   This calendar will also keep your nice words moving around so that you don't get comfortable in one area and become stuck in a rut. For instance, you might think your partner's hair is absolutely incredible, but if you say that every other day your partner begins to expect to hear about her hair and she no longer *really* hears what you say – those words have become old hat and just don't have much power within them anymore.

There are many times during the day that you can speak kind words to your partner. However, there are certain times, in my opinion, that are better than others. These are the times when such words will stick with your partner and make the most impact on his life and your relationship.

Morning is a great time. Words of love flow from you as the two of you are still in bed or maybe over breakfast. What a great way to start your day, hearing or speaking of something that brings a positive light to the day right from the start. Who wouldn't want to hear something that makes her feel wonderful right before she leaves to start her day?

Another great time is at lunch. If the two of you get to have lunch together, you could use that time to share kind and loving words with each other.

My favorite time, however, is right before bed –when you are lying in bed getting ready to shut the lights off and drift off to sleep. What a perfect time to speak kindly and lovingly to each other. This is such a comforting way to end your day. Whether it has been a stressful day or not you can find warmth in these kind words. What a wonderful way to enter slumber, thinking about how important you are to your partner. It is relaxing to hear and speak in this manner. With that warmth surrounding you, you might even sleep better.

It is so important to share kind and loving words with your partner in person. I know in this day and age that texting and email are great ways to communicate, but they don't have the personal feel that face-to-face communication has. Yet, I will also say that warm and heartfelt texts or emails or notes by the bed are beautiful messages too. Just don't let it become the only time you share your love with your partner. Technology can't replace a hug or simple hand-holding. Body heat is another reason that speaking kind words works better in person. Think about the heat that a body generates. Imagine being snuggled down in bed together. Wow, that is a warm and cozy place to be.

If you don't have habit of sharing warm words with each other face-to-face, doing it via text or email simply won't have the impact that it could have. Use emails and texts throughout the day and/or when you have different schedules or have to travel away from one another. When you have to be away from your partner for an extended period of time you can still speak kind words to her by using that technology. Phone calls are cheap now with the availability of cell phones and you can even use the video camera on your laptop to create messages with video attached to them. These devices give your messages a little more flair when you send them.

Speaking kind and loving words to your partner is a way to make him feel better, but can you benefit from these words as well? How does it make you feel to compliment your partner? Does it make you feel like a wonderful person? Does it fill you with a sense of pride? Or could it possibly have no effect on you? Well, the kind words you speak *will* make you a better person, and they will get you to view things in a different light. You can pretty much bet these kind words are having a positive effect on you. When you tell your partner she is beautiful you are not only building up her self-esteem, but you are reminding yourself that you really do think your partner is beautiful. This book might have to jog your memory a little bit, but it can also release the dam, and let those feelings flood over you again. Remember picking up your partner for a date or seeing him across the room during the early stages of your relationship. He simply glowed in your eyes. Why does that stop?

I will tell you why—because you let it. It is not just you. Most everyone does it. You get comfortable in your relationship. You have to deal with daily life and the excitement you once felt for you partner gets swept under the rug. When you see something or someone every day you don't get that zing in your heart like you did early on. Speaking kind words and reminding her and yourself about those feelings will soon start putting that glow back into your partner's aura again.

The format of this book will set you up on a routine of speaking kind words to each other. You will be prompted to use a specific area of focus on each and every day for thirty days. You can vary the category for each day, but you should still fall into the routine of hitting the same areas in the same order. This will help you prevent missing any areas. At first this might seem a little hard—trying to come up with kind words each and every day. Believe me, once you get into the swing of it you won't have to look so hard. These wonderful words will just come to you. If you feel like you are struggling, don't wait until the last minute to try and think something up. My suggestion would be to read what category you will be focusing on in the morning. This will give you the whole day to come up with an amazing stream of kind and loving words.

I cannot express enough how this will help in your relationship. What do you have to lose? Speaking kind words to each other cannot harm anything, and if nothing else they will get things out in the open.

This book contains fourteen categories so that you have a two-week routine before you start over again. The fourteen categories are appearance, personality, a task performed, others' views, passion, without/before you, dreams, sexual, support, heartfelt, change, encouragement, actions, and little things. Don't stress. Relax. You only have to focus on one category a day. I realize that sometimes you are going to get stuck and you might have to skip a section, but be true to yourself and your partner and go back to that category the next day. Sticking with the program is not the easiest thing to do, but once you get it down there will be no stopping you.

Below is a brief description of each category. This will give you an idea of what you will be looking for. On each day's assignment, however, you will find specific details on what to look for. So don't sweat it right now.

Appearance: Focus on your partner's physical features. Consider things like his eyes, her hair, his body, etc. You will be asked to focus on a specific area and to explain what you like about this part of your partner's appearance.

Personality: This category is based on your partner and his/her traits. Is your partner smart, funny, good with people? These are just a few areas that might get you thinking. Personality will help you dive deep into several of the reasons why you fell in love with this person in the first place. There is a list of personality traits in the back of this book to help you.

Tasks Your Partner Performs: This area can be as simple as the chores he does around the house. Taking out the garbage, doing the dishes, or keeping up on the laundry are a few to start with. Tasks can also include things she does at work or areas in the community that she helps out with, such as volunteer work or social work.

Other's Views of Your Partner: Focus on wonderful words that you have overheard others say about your partner. They don't have to be grand, but something that will show your partner that others think he is special and not just you. This will help show your partner the great impact she has on others.

Passion: Focus on areas that your partner takes great pride in. Does he take every chance he can to help out at your humane society or do things for the needy in your neighborhood? The passion category can include how your partner approaches your relationship. Does he buy you flowers? Does she leave you little notes on the table? These are passionate things you need to express to them.

Without/Before You: Focus on how much better your life is now that this person is in it. Compare your life before she was a part of it. It can also focus on changes you have made because he is in your life.

Dreams: These are images the two of you have about your future together. Things the two of you want to accomplish as a couple. Maybe it is moving to another state, retiring in a warm climate or just living out a lifelong dream. Pass along your dreams to your partner and include him as a major part of that dream.

Sexual: The sexual area covers a lot of ground in your private life. This is where you will express the things your partner does that drives you crazy (in a good way). Tell her the things that you love. This category promotes a strong and bonded physical relationship while helping the two of you share intimate details and fosters communication about a subject that many people have a hard time talking about.   Get over the fear of speaking about sex because if there is one person you should be able to talk to about sex, it is your partner.

Support: Encourage your partner to get out and do things that he isn't as comfortable doing as maybe he should be. Things like taking classes or learning a new skill or doing an activity he has never tried. Sometimes we all need a little push to get us going in the right direction. It's hard to take that first step. However, the support you give in your kind words can make all the difference in the world.

Heartfelt: This is where you tell your partner of things that really tugged at your heartstrings. Things you might be able to expand on are how she helped an older person load his/her groceries, or things that he has said or stories he has told to your kids or nieces/nephews. These are the things that almost make you cry when you see them happening.

Change: Every part of life has changes. It may include getting a new job, moving to a new house, or having a child come into your life or something less like having to change flights. When you speak kind words in this category you can tell how remarkably your partner has handled these changes. Change includes things that throw your life into another direction even if only for the moment, but it also includes sudden changes like the cancelled flight. These changes keep you on your toes.

Encouragement: Very similar to support, but this is the skill you use to get your partner to take that first step and step into something new. Things like going back to school, changing careers, or breaking free from something he has wanted to change for a long time.

Action: These are the things your partner does that she is not looking for credit for. She is a silent helper. It might include things like helping a family in need without desiring acknowledgement for the action. Whatever the reason, your partner wants to help, but doesn't want publicity for it.

Little Things: These are the actions your partner does that makes you smile. Simple little things like singing in the shower or dancing while cleaning the house are things that don't really mean anything other than the fact they make you smile. These also add character to your partner and separate her from others.

As we move forward in this book you will be asked to write down your kind words either in this book or on a notepad to reference from time to time. Try not to repeat yourself if you can avoid it. Keeping the log will also help you stay focused on the task being presented. Documentation is a great way to keep record of what you are doing and it really helps you stick with the subject. Kind words are very powerful because they help actions come to life.

After you stick with this practice for a while you will begin to start to do it naturally without thinking. Following this for 30 days will help you develop it into a habit, but I hope you will try it for longer – say four-six to months. You will soon find yourself remembering things to comment on later with kind words. You might even start to stock pile them and have to keep them in a journal. This way you won't forget them later when you need to recall them.

As you go about speaking kind and loving words you will soon find that while the kind words are to make your partner feel good they start making you see your partner in a different way. Instead of focusing on the negative things, as we so often do in our relationships, you will constantly be looking for the positive. Instead of screaming at him when he forget to do something, you will remember the other things he did that were positive. Ah, you will start to appreciate your partner and the things that she does for your relationship. You see—speaking kind words can improve your relationship from both sides.

We often go through life with blinders on—only seeing what we want to see. We hear what we want to hear and focus on what we want to focus on. The things that usually get our attention are the negative things. We just expect the positive things to get done without question or effort. If a person takes out the garbage every day for a year, then misses one day we automatically think about the day he failed to get the garbage out instead of the 364 days that he managed to get the garbage out without any problem. This is true across the board. Just watch the evening news. The majority of the news focuses on the negative. You may not be able to change the news, but you can change your relationship.

Think about your relationship. How many times have you overlooked the positive and focused on the negative? Well, you are about to break out of this rut. You are going to jump start your love and get it back on track. You are going to do it by using a system in which you tell your partner how wonderful and appreciated he/she is. How simple is that?

BEGIN SPEAKING NOW

DAY ONE

APPEARANCE

This is your very first day of speaking kind and loving words to your partner. I hope you are ready to transform your life and get your relationship moving in a better direction. The first topic is in my opinion the easiest of the bunch. Basically, what you have to look for is what attracted you to your mate in the first place. I am sure that most of you in the very beginning had a physical attraction to your mate. All you need to do here is open up and say what you are thinking. Pick the feature of your partner you find the most exciting and tell him that it makes you love him even more.

Example:

Looking him/her in the eyes, "Honey you have the most amazing eyes I have ever seen. From the very first time I saw you those eyes pulled me in. I could just sit and stare into your eyes for hours at a time."

Write your ideas for kind words here.

DAY TWO

PERSONALITY

I hope your first day of speaking kind words went well. On day two you are going to focus on your partner's personality. Pick a personality trait that you love about your partner. Maybe he is always happy or she is very humorous. You can find a list of personality traits at the end of this book if you feel stuck. Reflect on this personality trait in your partner. Think how it has been a wonderful asset in a situation. Give an example when you share your feelings with your partner. When you give specific examples of her personality traits you are showing that you are not just generalizing and that you actually feel this way.

Example:

"Honey, I can't believe how funny you are. You should be a comedian. The other night at the party, when you were talking about the lady with the funny hat, you had

everyone rolling on the floor. I love the laughter you bring

into the world."

Write your ideas for kind words here.

_____

_____

_____

_____

_____

_____

_____

_____

_____

_____

_____

_____

DAY THREE

TASKS YOUR PARTNER PERFORMS

When you are thinking about tasks your partner performs get out of the box a little. Don't go for the classic chores list. "Thank you for taking out the trash" only goes so far. Look deeper into your partner's make-up to see tasks that he performs, which maybe you don't acknowledge very often. Things like when she let you take your shower first to make sure you had hot water or when he goes out of his way to make you feel loved. These things happen a lot more than you realize. If you just open your eyes a little, you will find them everywhere you look.

Example:

"I want to thank you so much honey for taking Junior to the market with you today. The extra time you allowed me to gather my thoughts and bearings really did me

some good. I hope to be able to return the favor for you when

you need it."

Write your ideas for kind words here.

_____

_____

_____

_____

_____

_____

_____

_____

_____

_____

_____

_____

_____

DAY FOUR

OTHER'S VIEWS OF YOUR PARTNER

Speaking about how others view your partner is a little tougher than several of the other areas in this book. For starters, you may have to draw from your memory bank a time when someone spoke kindly about your partner. You should have specific examples and use people's names to make your partner's heart fill with warmth. Telling your partner what others find valuable in him will encourage him to do it more often and it will even help him form a bond with the person whom spoke so kindly about him. Some of the people you might get this information from include your family, co-workers, friends, and even teachers. You have to listen a little more closely to remember these examples for later use.

Example:

"You know little Billy's teacher was amazed by the way you interacted with the children today. He said that very seldom do the parents get that involved on a field trip and that he wished that all the parents of the kids in his class were that amazing."

Write your ideas for kind words here.

DAY FIVE

PASSIONATE

When you look for the passion in your partner you want to focus on more than just romantic passion. You want to see and feel the passions that she has in life. These passions can be just about anything and everything. Dance might be a passion of one person while baseball might be the other person's passion. You can always focus on the passion between the two of you, but that is covered a little later. I would like you to use the passion section to live and breathe the things your partner obviously has a passion for. Express your desire to understand or listen to his take on the subject.

Example:

"My beloved you are so passionate about dance. I love to watch you let go of yourself while you are watching the movement. How did that all come about?"

"It started when I was a young girl and my Grandmother saved for months to take me to see the New York City Ballet. Not only was I taken back by my Grandmother's action but, the ballet was the most amazing thing I can remember from my childhood. I can't believe I have never gone again"

Write your ideas for kind words here.

_____
_____
_____
_____
_____
_____
_____
_____
_____
_____
_____
_____

DAY SIX

WITHOUT/BEFORE YOU

Without/before you allows you to tell your partner how much he has impacted your life by telling him that without/before him you might have been doing something totally different. It is the classic before and after image that you want to portray here. Making sure that the after is way better than the before. Maybe you partner introduced you to a wonderful activity that you had no prior interest in. Maybe, your partner got you off a path of destruction and on one that has hope and a future. Spill your guts and let him know that you are very thankful for his love in your life.

Example:

"You know honey before you were in my life I did a lot of drinking. Once we met, I started seeing how wonderful life can be without being intoxicated. Thank you so much for

that. You know you probably added years to my life and I look forward to spending them with you."

Write your ideas for kind words here.

_____
_____
_____
_____
_____
_____
_____
_____
_____
_____
_____
_____
_____

DAY SEVEN

DREAMS

Speaking kind words about dreams are really quite simple. Just think about your own dreams and put your partner into them. Whether it be a dream you have for retirement or an achievement you want to accomplish put your lover smack dab in the middle of it so that she can share the dream with you. Long-term dreams seem to be the obvious ones, but try to think about ones that might happen sooner and include her in those also.

Example:

"You know I always wanted to run in a marathon. I have been training pretty hard and I think I am ready to enter my first one. I would love for you to be part of that, maybe in my support team or just being there when I cross the finish line would mean so much to me."

Write your ideas for kind words here.

DAY EIGHT

SEXUAL

Sexual kind and loving words are sometimes the most difficult to get out. It may be because one of you is shy or not very outspoken about your intimate times. When you speak these kinds word don't expect any rebuttal or response, just speak your mind and see what happens. You might spark a great conversation. If not, you are at least letting your partner know what you enjoy. Feel your partner out. Some people like to hear these kind words a little more graphically while some will just like the basics. Your culture and upbringing will have a lot of influence on how you accept or create these words. I suggest you say these things at a time separate from when you are beginning to make love or have just completed a love making session.

Example:

"Sweetie, you know the other night when you were under the covers giving me oral sex? Well, I just wanted to let you know it was you took me to a different planet. I felt incredible. Maybe next time I can return the favor."

Write your ideas for kind words here.
_____
_____
_____
_____
_____
_____
_____
_____
_____
_____
_____
_____

DAY NINE

SUPPORT

Being supportive to your partner is a must in a relationship. We all want confirmation that what we are doing is the right thing, but sometimes hearing it is the best way to feel it. You can be supportive to anything you partner does from exercising to going back to school. These things take commitment and dedication for your partner and from time to time might create a little stress for him. You want to validate him and his pursuit as much as you can. Joining him is one way, but telling him in an intimate setting will score big with him.

Example:

"Wow, I can't believe how well you are doing in that class you are taking. With all the other stuff you have going on you still find time to excel in your course work. I am truly amazed at your dedication."

Write your ideas for kind words here.

DAY TEN

HEARTFELT

In my opinion, this is one of the best areas for speaking kind words. In today's society we so often keep our feelings locked inside and don't share the important things that need to be shared. These are the things that make your eyes water or make you immediately hug your partner. For this section you will have to reach deep down inside yourself and pull up things that might be hard to unleash. These, heartfelt words are the ones that will help you by giving you the chance to express your deepest secrets to your partner.

Example:

"Darling, you have made me feel so wonderful throughout this pregnancy. I have to tell you, however, I am really scared that I won't be the best mother in the world. I am terrified that I will do something wrong or hurt the baby

in some way. But, with you as my rock I am sure we will have

the most wonderful memories to share with this child."

Write your ideas for kind words here.

_____

_____

_____

_____

_____

_____

_____

_____

_____

_____

_____

_____

_____

DAY ELEVEN

CHANGE

Changes are a fact of life. We need to embrace them as they come into our lives. However, this isn't always the easiest thing to do. As a partner and a lover you need to make sure you acknowledge the positive way that change is affecting your partner. She needs to hear that you know it was a challenge for her, but that you are proud of her for sticking with it.

Example:

"Sweetheart, I am amazed at the way you are handling the kids getting a pet rat. I know you were not totally on board when we decided that it was okay. However, I have seen you making great strides of acceptance for the rat. Just the other day, I noticed that you were not totally disgusted as the kids let Mr. Cheesy run across your shoulders."

Write your ideas for kind words here.

_____
_____
_____
_____
_____
_____
_____
_____
_____
_____
_____
_____

DAY TWELVE

ENCOURAGEMENT

When you speak kind words of encouragement you are being the rock to lean on for your partner. Maybe he is having a hard time deciding on a career change or having to decide on a life affecting issue. The basic premise of this is for you to encourage him to take the leap or to stay put, whatever fits your situation. Don't waiver or try to get him to change his mind. Be his rock.

Example:

"I know that deciding to leave the job that you loved in order to make more money was a hard one to make. I just want you to know that I am standing behind you 100%. I will be here if you need to talk or if you have a bad day at work. I just want you to know that your decision isn't as important as my love for you."

Write your ideas for kind words here.

_____
_____
_____
_____
_____
_____
_____
_____
_____
_____
_____
_____

DAY THRITEEN

ACTION

Your partner's actions give you ample opportunity to speak kind words. Look for things that she does that doesn't gain her any rewards except for the pleasure she gets from completing these tasks. Coaching youth groups, volunteering for charities, helping out the elderly lady down the street are all good examples of the actions I am talking about. The formula is simple—look for anything that requires work, but goes without pay.

Example:

"I am so impressed with the way you stepped up at the youth group yesterday. No one else was going to volunteer to stay all night with the youth sleepover. Those kids are very lucky you are such a wonderful person, and so am I."

Write your ideas for kind words here.

DAY FOURTEEN

SILLY

All you have to do to find silly actions that you can speak kind and loving words about is to make notes of times your partner makes you laugh or smile. Little things like telling jokes or when something unexpected happens that has you both rolling on the floor laughing. You need to thank your partner for putting laughter into your life.

Example:

"My love, I am so sorry that you slipped and dropped the birthday cake today. I was so glad that you didn't get hurt. You made my day with your reaction however. Most people would have cried about the cake, but with cake covering you the laughter you let out showed me and everyone else how wonderful you are."

Write your ideas for kind words here.

DAY FIFTEEN

APPEARANCE

Appearance is the most aggressive thing you can speak kind words about. For your second time of speaking kind and loving words about your partner's appearance make sure to avoid the past words on appearance you used. Find a completely different area of her appearance to compliment. The key here is to mix it up.

Example:

"Babe, I can't believe how beautiful your feet are. I mean the way you keep your toenails painted—my attention is drawn to them anytime you wear sandals or are barefoot."

Write your ideas for kind words here.

DAY SIXTEEN

PERSONALITY

Back on day two you spoke kind words to your partner about his personality. Two weeks later, you are about to do it again. Pick a different personality trait this time and run with it. Some people take great pride in their personality while others just let it flow naturally. The great thing about personality is that you can't fake it. If you're not funny, then you can't pretend to be. It just doesn't work. So make sure your words match your partner's personality. You are just setting yourself up for failure if the words you speak are untrue. Pull them from your heart and you can never go wrong.

Example:

"I cannot believe how observant you are. The other day when you got the license plate number of that car involved in the hit and run was amazing. Everyone else was

focused on the action and you, my darling, were more focused

than all of us. I am sure the owner of the parked car is really

thankful that you were so observant. You made the work for

the police a lot easier."

Write your ideas for kind words here.

_____

_____

_____

_____

_____

_____

_____

_____

_____

_____

_____

_____

DAY SEVENTEEN

TASKS YOUR PARTNER PERFORMS

Last time you spoke kind words to your partner about the tasks he performed I asked you to stay away from the chores list. Today I want you to focus on the great things your partner does around the house. Be it vacuum the carpet, do the laundry, or even cook supper. Tell him how much you appreciate his actions and let him know you don't take it for granted. These kind words go a long way because we all want to know that what we are doing is getting noticed and not just taken for granted.

Example:

"Thank you so much for getting all the laundry done last night. I sometimes forget how much work it is since you usually do it. Don't ever think I don't appreciate it. It truly is wonderful every time I go to the closet and find my clothes washed and hung there for me."

Write your ideas for kind words here.

_____

_____

_____

_____

_____

_____

_____

_____

_____

_____

_____

DAY EIGHTEEN

OTHER'S VIEWS OF YOUR PARTNER

By now, you are probably noticing things far more often that you can share with our partner. I hope you are listening to others and the way they speak of your partner. Get behind the scenes and listen to the way people talk. It might be someone that doesn't even know your partner. It can be something so small that even as her partner we forget it or seem to overlook the wonderful person she is. We only need to hear someone speak kindly of our partner to remind us.

Example:

"Last night at the party I overheard a couple of people talking about how funny you are. They were amazed at the quick wit you produced as the conversation went on. I sometimes overlook that quality in you, and just expect it because I know that is part of who you are."

Write your ideas for kind words here.

_____
_____
_____
_____
_____
_____
_____
_____
_____
_____
_____
_____

DAY NINETEEN

PASSION

Today is the day I want you to speak kind words about the passion your partner shows to you in your relationship. Last time, we focused on things that your partner was passionate about. Today focus on the passion he has towards you. I am still not talking about sex here. I want you to focus on what he is passionate about in regards to you. It is easy to get a little confused and think passion always leads to intimacy. Sometimes it just creates warm and fuzzy feelings.

Example:

"My beloved, last night I stumbled upon an email you left open from your friend in California. Usually, I try not to invade your privacy, but I caught a glimpse of my name in the email, which raised my curiosity. I can't tell you how wonderful I felt when I read the words you had written. How you talked about me made me blush with pride. The

wonderful things that you said showed me truly just how very much you love me. Again, I am sorry about the invasion of your privacy, but not about my feelings that mirror yours."

Write your ideas for kind words here.

_____
_____
_____
_____
_____
_____
_____
_____
_____
_____
_____
_____

DAY TWENTY

WITHOUT/BEFORE YOU

We all wonder about the "what if's"—those things in life that we chose and how they would had been different if we would have chosen differently. You cannot go back and change things or see how they would have turned out. However, you can confirm to your partner just how much you feel you made the right choice with her. By sharing loving words about how you feel your life would have been different without her.

Example:

"Things have been a little tough around here lately, as you well know. I wanted to let you know how truly blessed I am that you are here with me. The tough times seem way more bearable with you. Alone, I don't know how I would have faced these fears, but with you by my side I feel there is nothing we can't handle together."

Write your ideas for kind words here.

DAY TWENTY-ONE

DREAMS

Make an elaborate plan for your future together. Talk about being wealthy and leading an exciting life. Give specific details as to paint a picture for your partner. Let her know you are planning on giving the two of you the finest things in life. Dream up the biggest picture you can for the two of you and set that energy in motion. Express these sweet words as if there is no doubt that they will happen. Allow your partner to join in on these dreams adding her own touches from time to time, after all these dreams involve both of you.

Example:

"You know, sweetie, when we get that house in Hawaii and we have even more time to spend together, I think we should hire a yoga trainer to come to our house and teach us yoga on the beach. When my book hits the best seller's list we will make sure to take time to fly to all the exotic places

we can. I want you right by my side when we have to attend all

the press functions and parties. That way I can tell them how

important you have been to my creative process. Plus they

will want to see all the amazing artwork you produce from

your studio."

Write your ideas for kind words here.
_____
_____
_____
_____
_____
_____
_____
_____
_____
_____
_____
_____
_____

DAY TWENTY-TWO

SEXUAL

Speaking kind words about sex can start out being flirtatious. You can use it as foreplay to get your motors running. Bragging about your partner's sexual organs or about his ability in bed might make him blush. However, it will more than likely make him swell with pride. When you are speaking these kind words you can use your hands to make dramatic points and heighten his excitement. Talk a little dirty and see if you get some instant acknowledgement to your comments.

Example:

When we make love you make me feel so wonderful. Sometimes I feel like the world has stopped and we are floating in space. Do you want to go there with me now?"

Write your ideas for kind words here.

DAY TWENTY-THREE

SUPPORT

Supportive kind words don't always require praise. Sometimes you can be supportive when the chips are down. Life is not a bed of rose petals and sometimes bad things happen. This is when your compassionate and loving words can work wonderful magic. Things such as deaths in the family, losing a job, fights with friends are just a few of the examples that can have the sting taken out of them by your love and compassion. Be supportive. Don't second guess your partner's actions. Focus on the positive things that she has done and avoid questioning her judgment.

Example:

"Sweetheart, you know you didn't like that job anyway. They are going to be so sorry that they let you go. How many times have you come home frustrated? Now

maybe you can find a job that really makes you feel good.

There is a silver lining in every storm cloud!"

Write your ideas for kind words here.

_____

_____

_____

_____

_____

_____

_____

_____

_____

_____

_____

_____

_____

DAY TWENTY-FOUR

HEARTFELT

Again, as you start to figure out the best heartfelt words to say all you need to do is open up your heart and let your feelings come out. Look for times that your partner has picked you up when you were down or how she carried you through some rough times. Challenge yourself to find something that you feel will really hit home with her—something that will make her heart light up. When you speak these words to her, make sure to look deep into her eyes. You want to let her know this is coming from your heart.

Example:

"You know the other day at the little league game when I pulled our best player out of the game because of his bad attitude. All the other parents were mad because we lost the game. However, you knew I did the right thing and supported my decision and let the other parents know why.

That reminded me how wonderful our bond is. When all the other parents were focused on winning, you and I knew there was so much more at stake. Hopefully, we made a difference in that young man's life and showed all the kids that winning isn't everything!"

Write your ideas for kind words here.

_____
_____
_____
_____
_____
_____
_____
_____
_____
_____
_____
_____
_____
_____

DAY TWENTY-FIVE

CHANGE

Changes are the spice of life. They keep us from getting stuck in the same pattern. They are the curves that come at us and then drift away as we get past them. Being able to be open to changes as they arise in your relationship is an important part of making your relationship a lasting one. Never let your first opinion of the change come blurting out of your mouth. Give it time to digest and then once the initial shock of it is over you will be able to find the positive in it. Changes can range from changing your hair color to switching careers at what seems like a bad time. Look for the good when you speak your loving words about the changes that have hit your life.

Example:

"It was really a shock to me today to come home and see you with red hair. You have had blond hair since the day

we met. It took me a while to get used to it, but now I must
say it makes me want to get to know you all over again. It is
so drastically different from you previous hair color that I
find it a little exotic. It makes me look at you in a whole
different light. Knowing you're still the same person on the
inside, this change lets me find you all over again on the
outside!"

Write your ideas for kind words here.
_____
_____
_____
_____
_____
_____
_____
_____
_____
_____
_____
_____

Encouragement sometimes means pushing a little to get someone motivated. Some of us will spend forever debating if we should take the leap into something new. When this happens we might waste a lot of valuable time, even years, while pondering if it is the right choice to make. Expressing your kind and loving words can offer the power for your partner to take the leap of faith with the knowledge that you are behind her one hundred percent. That little support can sometimes be the event that makes or breaks a person's dreams.

Example:

"You know, sweetie, I know you have always regretted not getting your college degree. I think that the time is right for you to follow that dream now. You are between jobs, and I am making enough money to support us. Sure, we

will have to be careful, but think of the upside when you are finished with school. I would love to see you follow through on that dream!"

Write your ideas for kind words here.

DAY TWENTY-SEVEN

ACTION

You have surely heard the old saying that actions speak louder than words. This is so true; therefore, your kind words should speak wonderfully of the actions you partner has performed. When you are thinking of things for this section look for the out-of-the-ordinary things your partner does. Things like taking off work a little early to spend with the kids or getting up early to pack the car for vacation so that everyone else can sleep a little longer. These are the type of actions that are not usually even thought about, but mean so much to us.

Example:

"Honey I noticed that you spent all night up tracking the storm that was near us last night. You must have been up until 2 A.M. watching to make sure we were safe. I must say I find that rather attractive in you. You are so protective of us, your family. Even though we don't see that type of love it

makes me feel even closer to you knowing that we mean so

much to you."

Write your ideas for kind words here.

_____

_____

_____

_____

_____

_____

_____

_____

_____

_____

_____

_____

_____

DAY TWENTY-EIGHT

SILLY

When your partner does something to put a smile on your face that is the silliness you want to comment on later in the evening or if the time is right share loving and kind words right then. It might be something like he misunderstood the instructions you gave him and did the totally wrong thing or that she forgot to take her drink off the top of the car as she drove off to work. These are the funny little things that make your life so wonderful. Anytime you partner causes a smile to grace your face make note of it and let him know about it later.

Example:

"I have to tell you that today when you were going to water the lawn and you set the sprinkler beside the sidewalk. I know you waited until the kids were getting off the bus to turn it on. I saw you watching from around the house and then right as they got within range you let them have it.

Sitting inside watching all this I burst out laughing watching our children suddenly consumed by the sudden rain from the sprinkler. Watching you come running out laughing at them as they chased you made my heart sing. You bring so much joy into our life. Don't ever stop being that silly."

Write your ideas for kind words here.

_____

_____

_____

_____

_____

_____

_____

_____

_____

_____

_____

_____

DAY TWENTY-NINE

BONUS DAY 1

Today is your day to pick from the list of things you want to speak kind words about. If you can't decide, then throw them all into a hat and pick one out. You should be getting quite used to speaking kind words by now so you shouldn't have any problem locating things to address. Let you heart guide you to the area you feel your partner needs to hear more about. Make sure not to repeat any of the other kind words you have used this month. Below is a list of the categories again. Circle the one you are going to use and have at it. You should be getting adjusted to this habit by now.

Choose one:

Appearance—Personality—Tasks Performed— Others View of Them—Passion— Without/Before You—Dream—Sexual—

Support—Changes—Encouragement—

Action—Silly

Write your ideas for kind words here.

_____

_____

_____

_____

_____

_____

_____

_____

_____

_____

_____

_____

DAY THIRTY

BONUS DAY 2

Again today you are going to get to pick from the list below. I still do not want you to repeat anything you have mentioned this month. You can really get creative and combine two categories if you like. Two that are easy to combine might include the appearance category and the sexual category. Yet, if you reflect back to the last silly example, you might mention how funny your partner is and how you loved her beautiful auburn hair blowing in the breeze while she waited to drench the kids. So many of these can feed off of the other and make for some interesting choices. Just remember to keep speaking these kind words. Your partner deserves it.

Choose one:

Appearance—Personality—Tasks Performed—Others View of Them—Passion—

Without/Before You—Dream—Sexual—

Support—Changes—Encouragement—

Action—Silly

Write your ideas for kind words here.

_____
_____
_____
_____
_____
_____
_____
_____
_____
_____
_____
_____

Well you have done it. You have managed to speak kind words for thirty full days. How does it feel? I am sure if you ask your partner he/she will tell you how great if feels. Love when left alone acts a lot like a plant—it starts to wither and die, but if you add water and sunlight it springs back to life. The kind words you are speaking are like water and sunlight to your relationship. These words go so much deeper than just affecting your love. You can build confidence in your partner for him to achieve more, and if that weren't enough, it builds a sense of worth inside you knowing that you can make someone feel special just by talking lovingly and kindly to her. Are you starting to see how much power you have in your voice and mind?

As you start to understand how powerful the gift of words is, can you start to see how this can make a difference outside your relationship, also? What about your employees or co-workers? Could they be affected by this simple act of speaking kind words? How about your children? Kind words can be so powerful to a young mind. If you think about it kind words can improve any situation. How about your little league team? Could they benefit from kind words, rather than yelling and screaming about things they did wrong? Heck even your pets can benefit from you speaking kind words to them. They understand more than you think.

If you start speaking compassionately and kindly all the time, how are people going to view you? People will definitely want to be around the new you, and why not? We all desire to hear kind words.

The ultimate purpose of this little book is to improve your relationship with the one you love. However, take these actions and spread them out to others. Speaking kind words is contagious.

When is the last time you said something nice to someone and they said something nasty back to you? That doesn't happen very often. When you are confronted with a nice statement about yourself, you relax and enjoy it. The tension decreases and you are put at ease. Even if you are angry with the person, it makes it very difficult to fire off when he/she is showing you kindness and compassion.

We all want to be appreciated and kind words are an acknowledgement of that appreciation. They pick us up and dust us off when we are having a bad day. Yet, sometimes we find ourselves yearning to hear them only to have our ears fall on a deafening silence. Perhaps, we should not desire those kind words, but they sure do make a difference in our lives. Those powerful little words can change our mood. Two of the greatest kind words in our language are, "Thank You."

Yes, those two small words can pack a potent punch. That is often enough recognition to satisfy our thirst and to help us bask in our glory.

While love is the feeling that we desire in life, kind words are the indication that we are loved.   As we claw and scratch our way through life it is nice to hear from time to time, "Hey you are doing a great job!"   Or, in the case of your relationship it might sound like this, "I love you so much."

Keep up on your kind words. Next time you hear someone speaking not so nicely to someone else, hand them a copy of this book and see if it makes a change in them.

Peace and love be with you my new friends.

Personality Traits

This is by no way a complete listing of traits, but it will get you started.

Accountable	Balanced
Active	Brave
Adaptable	Brilliant
Adventurous	Calm
Affable	Candid
Affectionate	Captivating
Agreeable	Careful
Alert	Caring
Altruistic	Charming
Analytical	Cheerful
Appropriate	Circumspect
Articulate	Clean
Artistic	Clearheaded
Assertive	Clever
Astute	Collaborative
Athletic	Comfortable
Attentive	Commanding
Attractive	Committed
Aware	Compassionate

Competitive	Educated
Concise	Efficient
Confident	Engaged
Conscious	Enterprising
Considerate	Enthusiastic
Constructive	Entrepreneurial
Content	Erudite
Courageous	Evenhanded
Coordinated	Expressive
Cooperative	Fair
Courteous	Faithful
Creative	Flexible
Curious	Fluent
Decisive	Focused
Dedicated	Forgiving
Dependable	Friendly
Determined	Fun
Devoted	Funny
Direct	Generous
Disarming	Genius
Disciplined	Gentle
Driven	Giving
Eager	Good

Graceful	Joyful
Grateful	Just
Gregarious	Kind
Handsome	Leader
Hard-working	Likable
Hardy	Logical
Healthy	Loving
Helpful	Loyal
Honest	Loyalty
Humble	Lucky
Imaginative	Mannered
Independent	Masculine
Industrious	Mature
Influential	Methodical
Informed	Moderate
Innovative	Modest
Insightful	Motivated
Inspired	Motivating
Inspiring	Neat
Intelligent	Noble
Interested	Nurturing
Intuitive	Objective
Involved	Observant

Omnipotent	Relaxed
Open	Reliable
Open-minded	Resourceful
Optimistic	Respected
Orderly	Respectful
Organized	Responsible
Original	Responsive
Passionate	Results-oriented
Patient	Secure
Perceptive	Self-aware
Personable	Self-controlled
Photogenic	Self-directed
Poised	Self-disciplined
Polite	Selfless
Positive	Self-reliant
Practical	Self-starter
Precise	Sensitive
Productive	Sensual
Professional	Serious
Punctual	Shrewd
Quick study	Sincere
Realistic	Skilled
Receptive	Sober

Sociable

Sociable

Independent

Socially conscious

Spiritual

Steady

Stoic

Striving

Strong

Subtle

Surprising

Sweet

Sympathetic

Systematic

Talented

Telegenic

Tenacious

Thorough

Tolerant

Trusting

Trustworthy

Unflappable

Un-intimidated

Unpretentious

Unselfish

Upstanding

Versatile

Visionary

Willing

Your Partner's Traits Brainstorm Page

When your partner walks into a room he is _____

_____

_____

When your partner shops for gifts for others she _____

_____

_____

When your partner is running late for work he _____

_____

_____

When you are ill your partner _____

_____

_____

When there is a problem your partner is _____

_____

_____

These are just to get you started. I want you to pay attention and think as you observe your partner throughout the day.

New Words Brainstorm Pages

A great way to give your relationship a boost is to change the language you use. Use different words than you typically use. Do you often say, "I love you,"? Change it occasionally to something like, "I adore you." or "I find you irresistible." Below you will find a list of suggestions and room for you to brainstorm. You might even consider speaking to your partner in a different language. You don't know a second language? No problem, jump online and search phrases such as "I love you" in Spanish or whatever language you want to learn that phrase in. You will also be able to obtain the audio pronunciation; you will amaze your partner with your new way of expressing your love.

Love—adoration, devotion, affection, tenderness, passion, ardor, enchantment, cherish, rapture,

What other words can you think of that might describe "love" or the meaning of "love"?_____

_____

_____

_____

_____

Beautiful —alluring, pretty, gorgeous, breath-taking, handsome, sexy, shimmering, dazzling, marvelous, radiant

What other words can you think of that might describe "beautiful" or the meaning of "beautiful"?_____

_____

_____

_____

_____

Endearments—dear, my love, my beloved, sweetheart, snuggle bunny, lover, best friend, honey

Your turn. _____

_____

_____

_____

Thankful—grateful, appreciative, content, pleased, obliged, respectful

Other words or ways your partner shows her gratitude _____

_____

_____

_____

Hello/Good-bye—Aloha, howdy, ciao, arrivederci, shalom, greetings, what's up,

Your turn. _____

_____

_____

_____

Sex—making love, being intimate, getting it on,
knocking boots, fool around, have relations

Your turn. _____

_____

_____

_____

Talk—chat, converse, discuss, communicate,
verbalize, gab

Your turn. _____

_____

_____

_____

Date—rendezvous, go out, keep company, court, romantic evening, special time

Your turn. _____

_____

_____

_____

Work/chores—effort, task, endeavor, performance, skill, obligation, specialization

Your turn. _____

_____

_____

_____

Now think of the other words you use to describe your partner and mix them up a bit. This will keep both of you on your toes.

A short list of phrases in different languages

My love
- French—mon amour
- Spanish—mi amor
- Italian—il mio amore

I love you
- French—je t'aime
- Spanish—te quiero
- Italian—l'amo

You are so beautiful
- French—tu es si belle
- Spanish—eres tan bella
- Italian—sei cosi bella

Thank you
- French—merci
- Spanish—gracias
- Italian—grazie

Sweet dreams
- French—doux rêves
- Spanish—dulces sueños
- Italian—sogni d'oro

Kiss me
- French— m'embrasser
- Spanish—bésame
- Italian—baciarmi

Note the category & if you completed this day.

One Month of
Kind & Loving Words

Day	Day	Day	Day	Day	Day	Day
1	2	3	4	5	6	7
7	8	9	10	11	12	13
14	15	16	17	18	19	20
21	22	23	24	25	26	27
28	29	30			Sample Tasks ☺ √	Sample Views ☹ not done

Recap

Day 1 – Appearance
Day 2 – Personality
Day 3 – Tasks Your Partner Performs
Day 4 – Other's Views of Your Partner
Day 5 – Passion
Day 6 – Without/Before You
Day 7 – Dreams
Day 8 – Sexual
Day 9 – Support
Day 10 – Heartfelt
Day 11 – Change
Day 12 – Encouragement
Day 13 – Action
Day 14 – Little Things

Day 15 – Appearance
Day 16 – Personality
Day 17 – Tasks Your Partner Performs
Day 18 – Other's Views of Your Partner
Day 19 – Passion
Day 20 – Without/Before You
Day 21 – Dreams
Day 22 – Sexual
Day 23 – Support
Day 24 – Heartfelt
Day 25 – Change
Day 26 – Encouragement
Day 27 – Action
Day 28 – Little Things

Day 29 & Day 30 –Bonus –pick you own category

Watch for our upcoming releases —

Dream Journal
Meditation Journal
Yoga Journal
Reasons to Smile
The Spirit of the Couple

Visit Rob and Janelle Alex 's website
www.inwardoasis.com